EASY PIANO

CHRIS TOMLIN
AND IF OUR GOD IS FOR US...

T0085253

Original Album Design by Jesse Owen

ISBN 978-1-61774-126-5

Hal•Leonard CORPORATION

7777 W. BLUEMOUND RD. P.O. BOX 13819 MILWAUKEE, WI 53213

Visit Hal Leonard Online at
www.halleonard.com

OUR GOD

Words and Music by CHRIS TOMLIN,
JESSE REEVES, MATT REDMAN
and JONAS MYRIN

With power

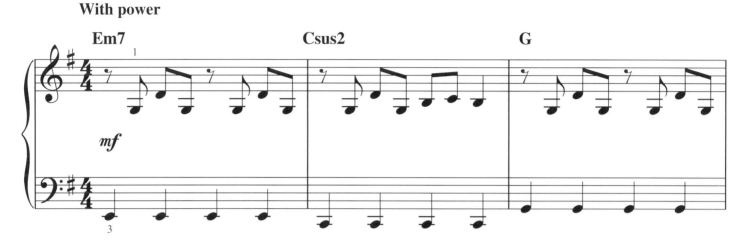

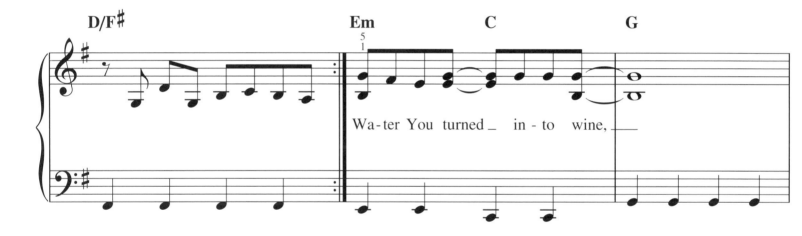

Wa-ter You turned _ in - to wine, _

o-pened the eyes _ of the blind. _ There's no one like You, _

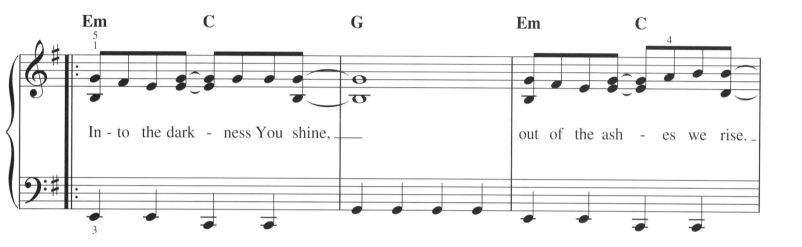

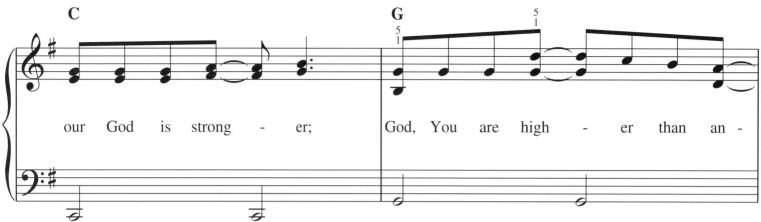

our God is strong – er; God, You are high – er than an –

– y oth – er. Our God is Heal – er, awe-some in pow – er, our God, ___

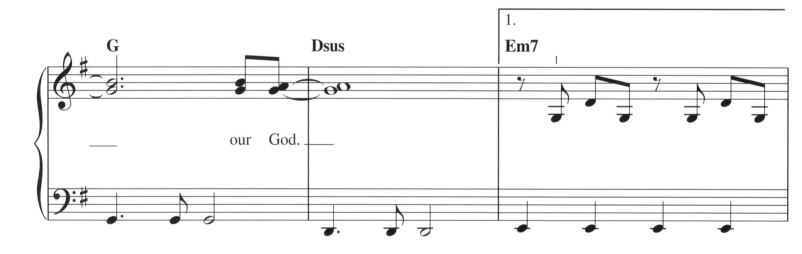

___ our God. ___

1.

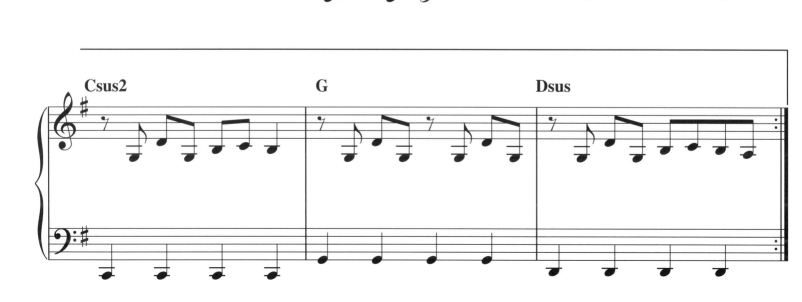

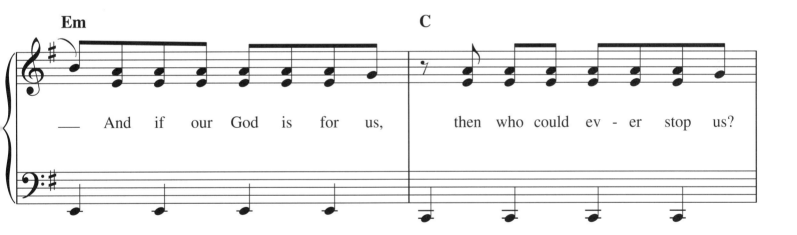

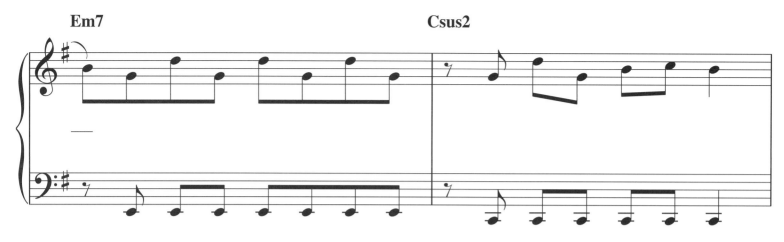

Then what could stand a - gainst? _

To Coda ⊕

D.S. al Coda
(take 2nd ending)

CODA ⊕

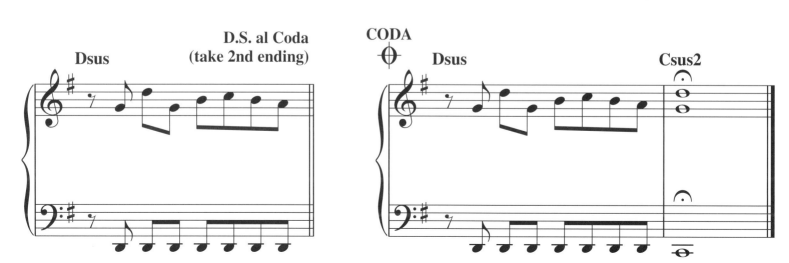

I LIFT MY HANDS

Words and Music by CHRIS TOMLIN,
LOUIE GIGLIO and MATT MAHER

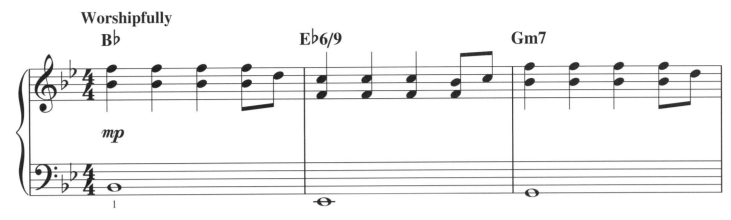

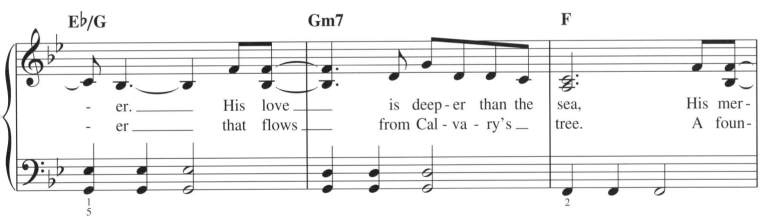

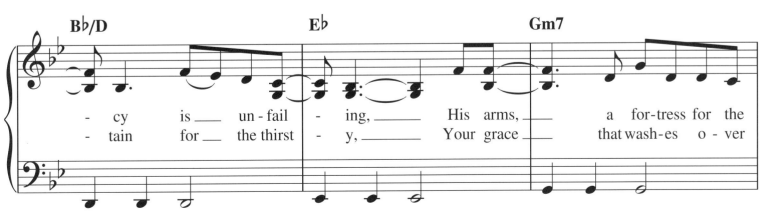

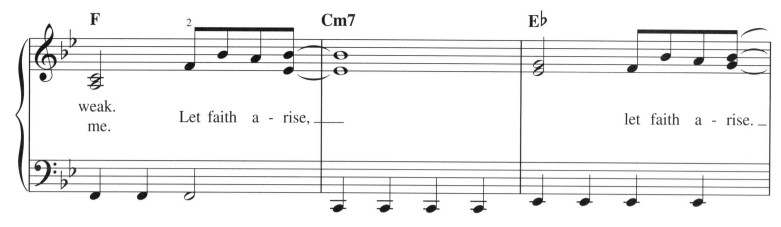

weak.
me.
Let faith a - rise, ___ let faith a - rise. ___

I lift my hands ___ to be - lieve a - gain.

You are my ref - uge, You ___ are my strength. ___ As I pour out my heart, ___

___ these things ___ I re-mem - ber: ___ You are faith - ful, God, ___ for-ev-

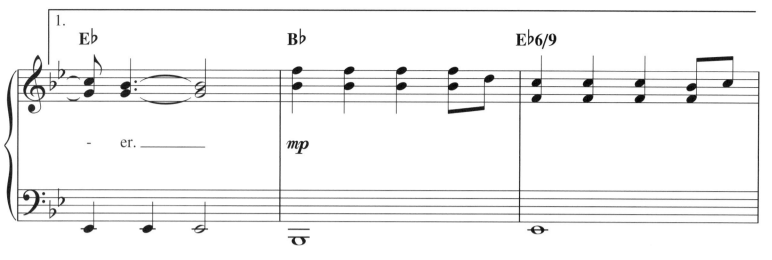

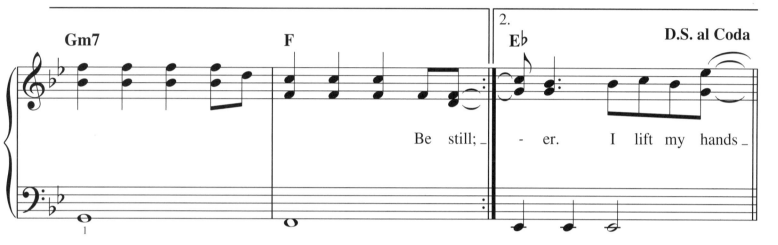

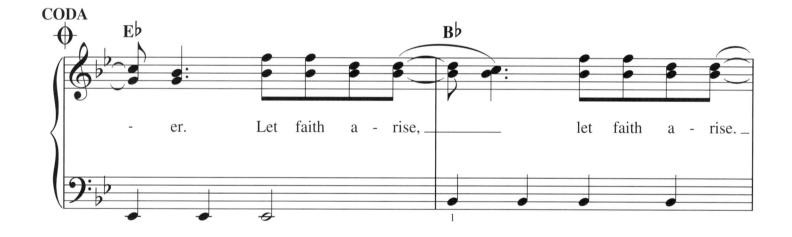

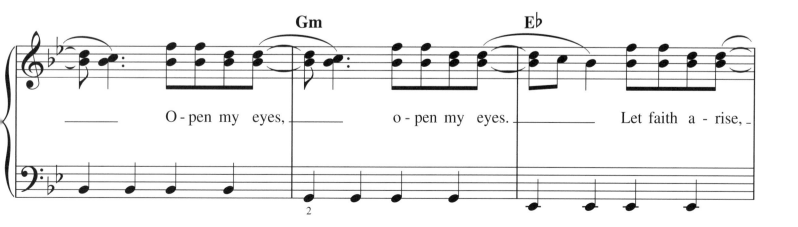

let faith a - rise. _____ O - pen my eyes, _____ o - pen my eyes. _____

_____ I lift my hands _____ to be - lieve a - gain. _____

_____ You are my ref - uge, You ___ are my strength. _____ As I pour out my heart, ___

_____ these things ___ I re - mem - ber: _____ You are faith - ful, God, ___ for - ev -

- er. I lift my hands _ - ful, God, _ You're faith - ful, God, _ for-ev-

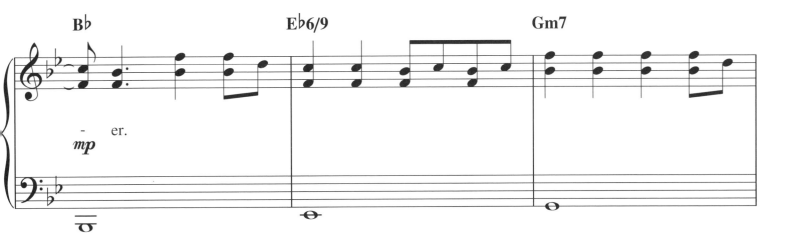

- er.

mp

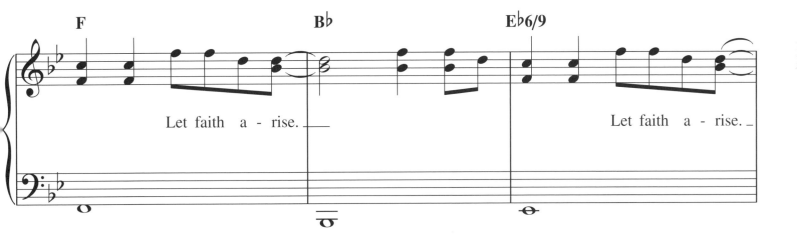

Let faith a - rise. _ Let faith a - rise. _

rit.

I WILL FOLLOW

Words and Music by CHRIS TOMLIN,
REUBEN MORGAN and JASON INGRAM

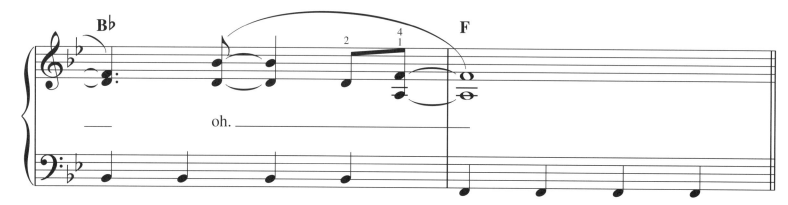

High - er than my sight, ___ high a - bove my life, ___
You're the One I seek, ___ know - ing I will find ___

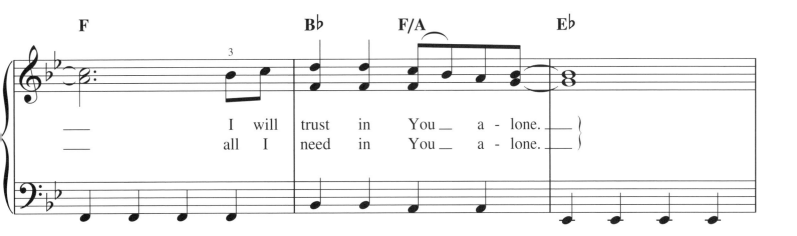

___ I will trust in You ___ a - lone. ___
___ all I need in You ___ a - lone. ___

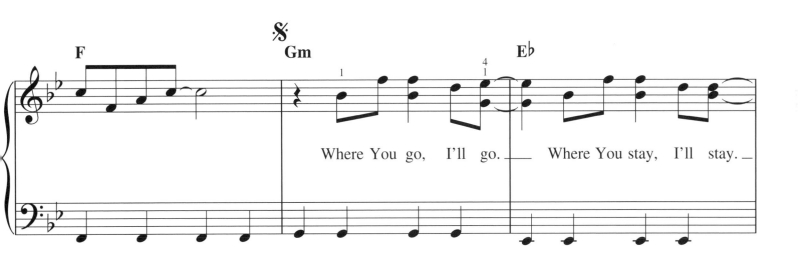

Where You go, I'll go. ___ Where You stay, I'll stay. ___

When You move, I'll move. ___ I will fol - low You. ___

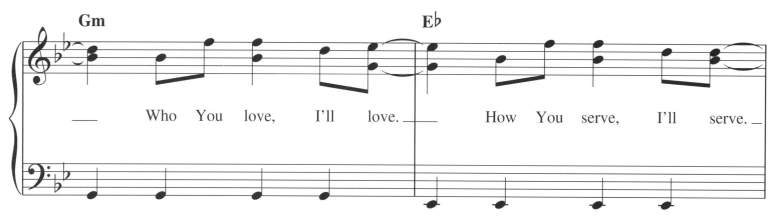

Gm ... **E♭**

Who You love, I'll love. How You serve, I'll serve.

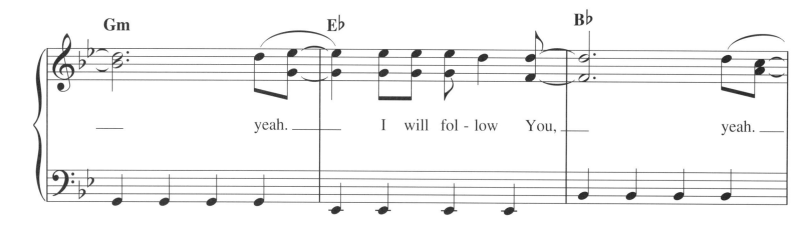

B♭ ... **F** ... **To Coda** ⊕

If this life I lose, I will fol-low You,

Gm ... **E♭** ... **B♭**

yeah. I will fol-low You, yeah.

1. **F**

2. **F** ... **E♭maj7**

In You, there's

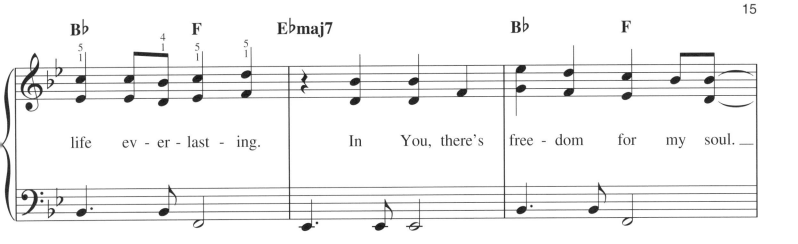

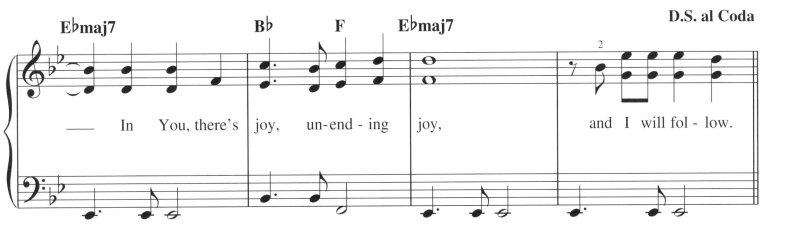

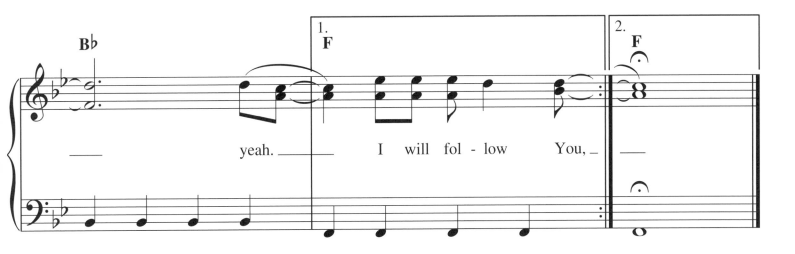

MAJESTY OF HEAVEN

Words and Music by CHRIS TOMLIN,
JESSE REEVES and MATT REDMAN

With a strong beat

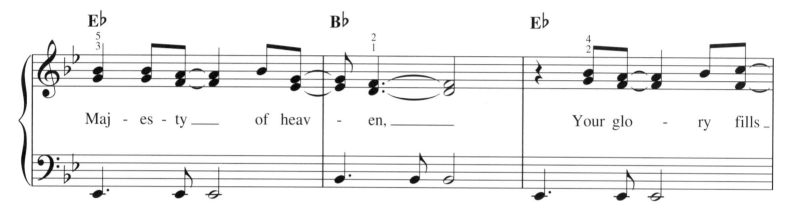

Maj - es - ty ___ of heav - en, ___ Your glo - ry fills ___

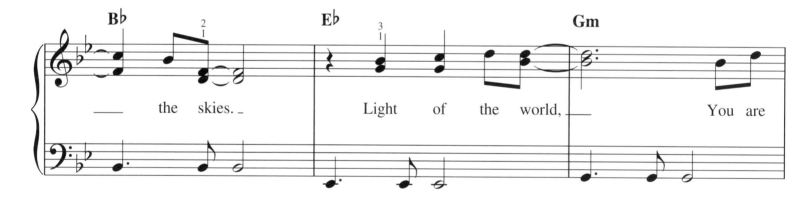

___ the skies. ___ Light of the world, ___ You are

Lord of all.

Hum - bled by ___ Your pres -
Mer - ci - ful ___ and might-

- ence, _____ a - mazed _ by who _ You are. _____
- y, _____ my heart _ is o - ver - whelmed. _

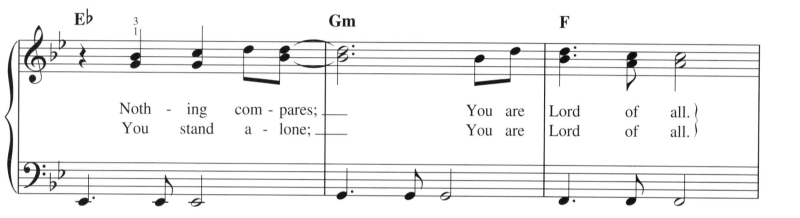

Noth - ing com - pares; _ You are Lord of all.
You stand a - lone; _ You are Lord of all.

To You the na - tions bow _ down, _ to You cre-

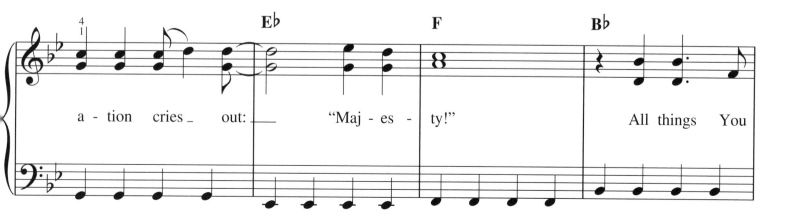

a - tion cries _ out: _ "Maj - es - ty!" All things You

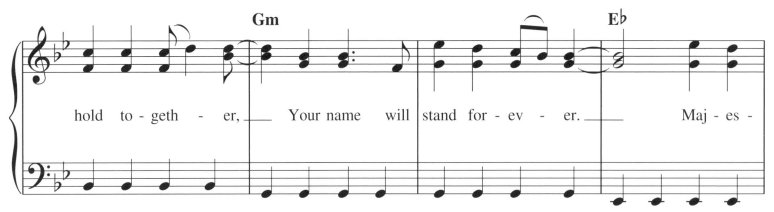

hold to - geth - er,___ Your name will stand for - ev - er.___ Maj - es -

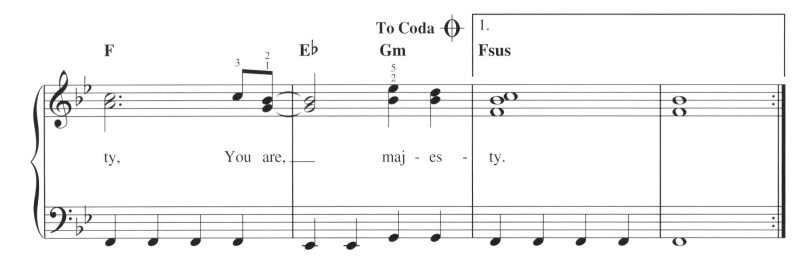

ty, You are,___ maj - es - ty.

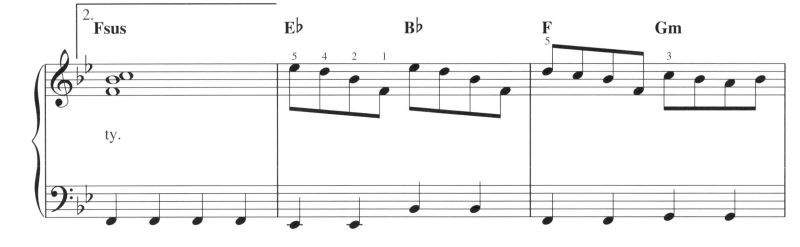

ty.

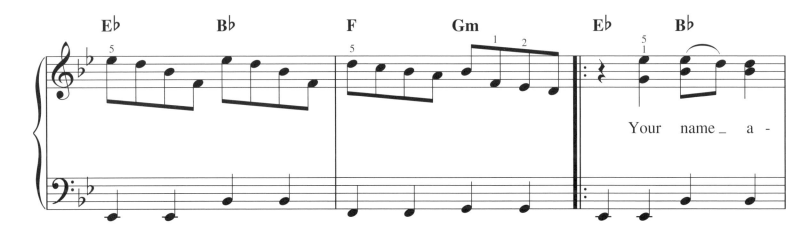

Your name _ a -

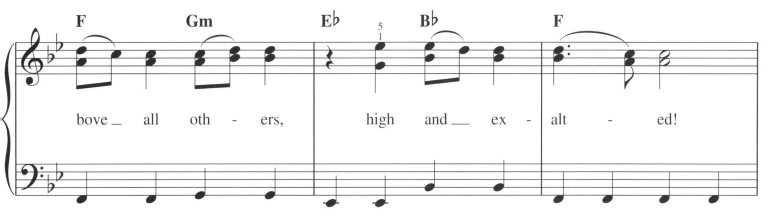

bove ___ all oth - ers, high and ___ ex - alt - ed!

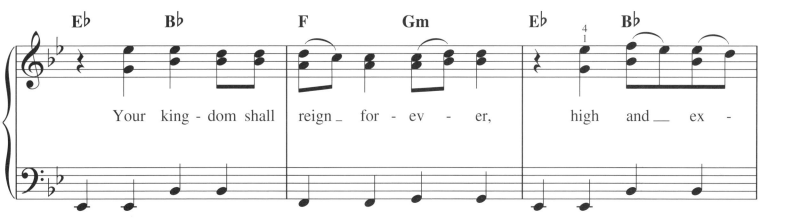

Your king - dom shall reign ___ for - ev - er, high and ___ ex -

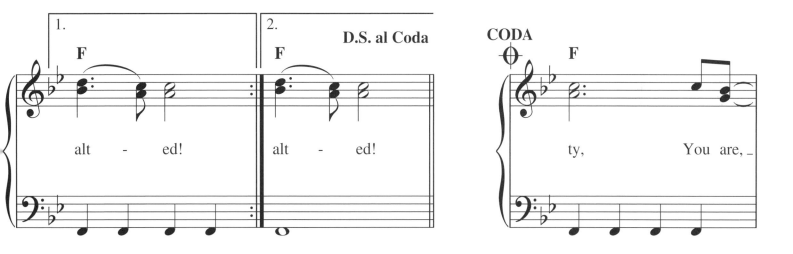

1.
alt - ed!

2. D.S. al Coda
alt - ed!

CODA
ty, You are, ___

___ maj - es - ty.

NO CHAINS ON ME

Words and Music by CHRIS TOMLIN,
JESSE REEVES and MATT REDMAN

This is a dream,

a dream for the world ___ to see ___ You, ___ a dream for the world ___
now is the time ___ for free - dom, ___ a - ban - don my cold

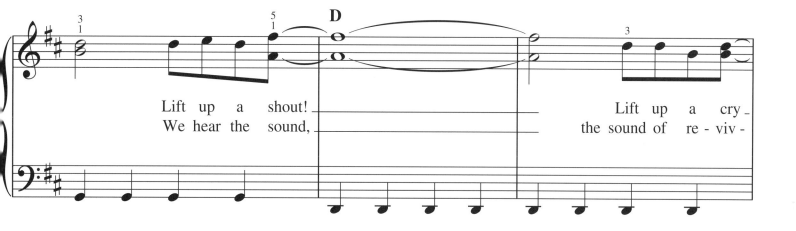

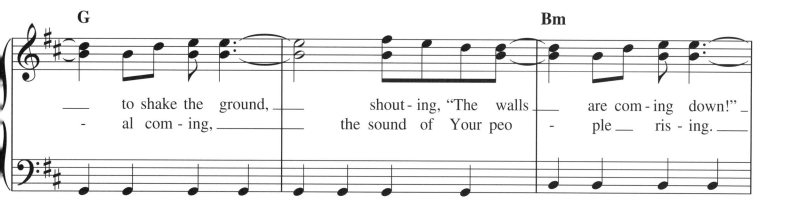

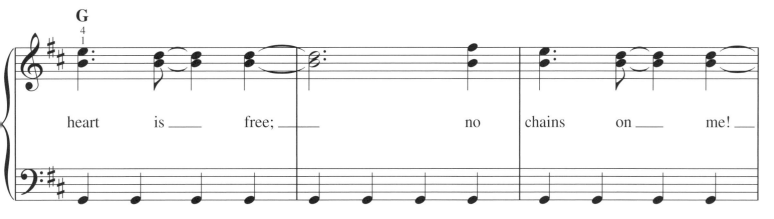

heart   is   free;   no   chains   on   me!

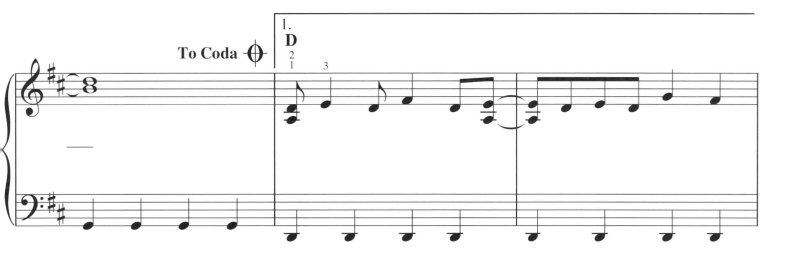

To Coda ⊕ | 1.

Now is the time,   Oh,   oh,   oh,

2.

oh, oh.   Oh, oh, oh,   oh, oh. The

23

walls are com-ing down, the walls are com-ing down,

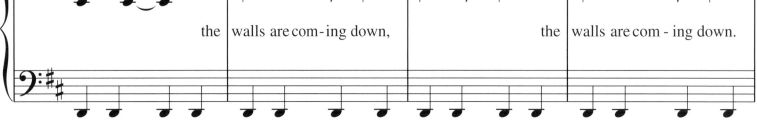

the walls are com-ing down, the walls are com-ing down.

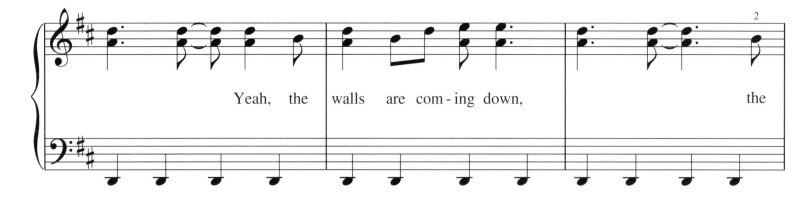

Yeah, the walls are com-ing down, the

walls are com-ing down. _____ Like a roll-

D.S. al Coda

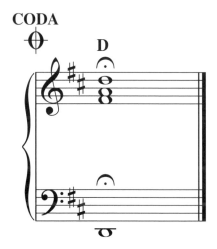

CODA

FAITHFUL

Words and Music by CHRIS TOMLIN,
CHRISTY NOCKELS, NATHAN NOCKELS
and ED CASH

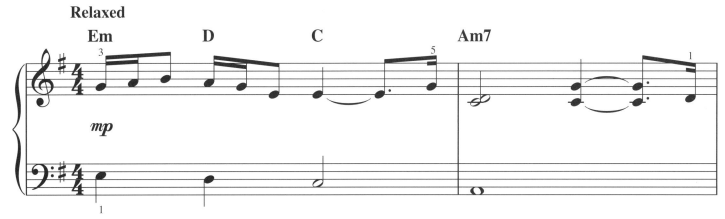

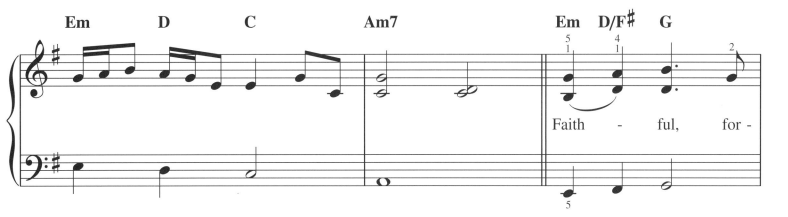

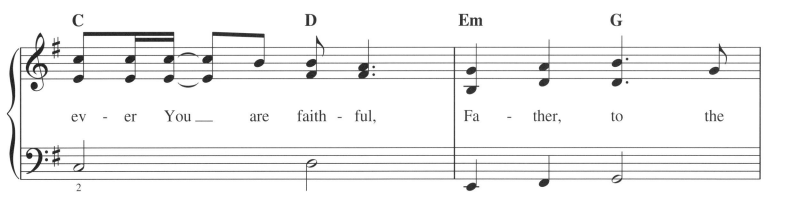

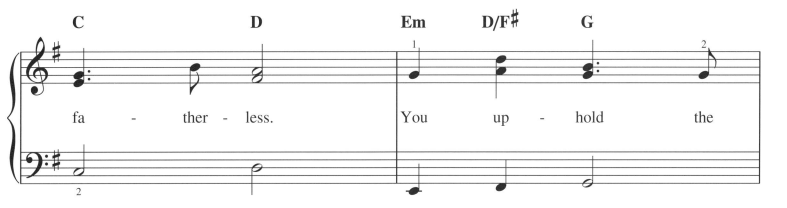

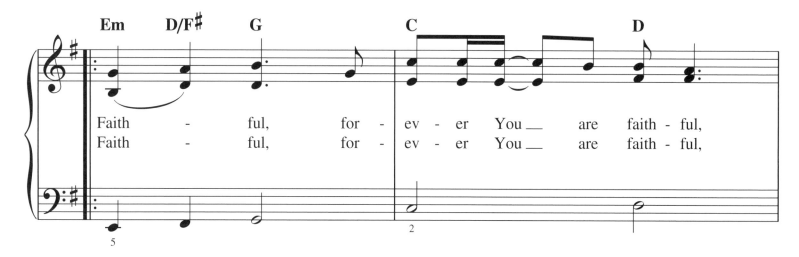

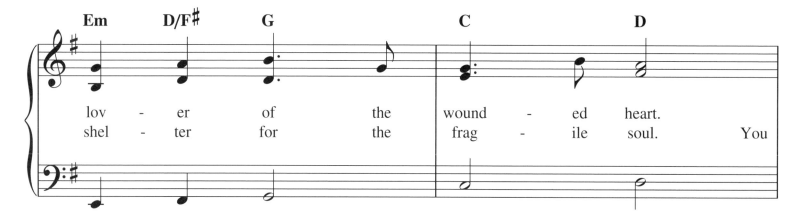

You are faith - ful, God. _____ And I will
You are faith - ful, God. _____

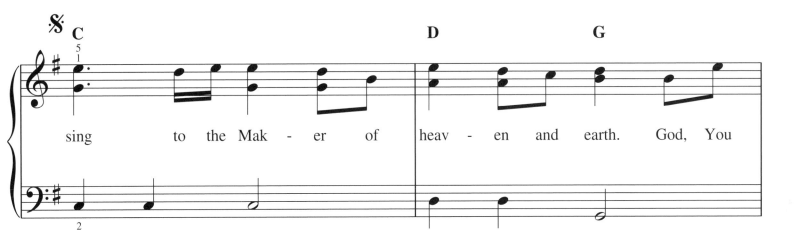

sing to the Mak - er of heav - en and earth. God, You

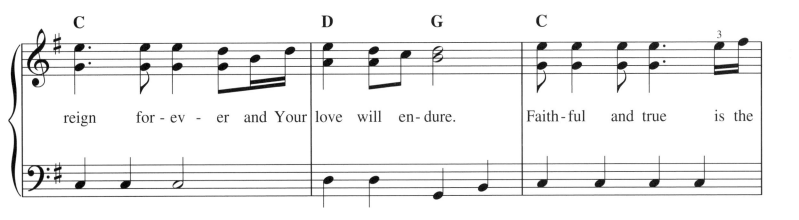

reign for - ev - er and Your love will en - dure. Faith - ful and true is the

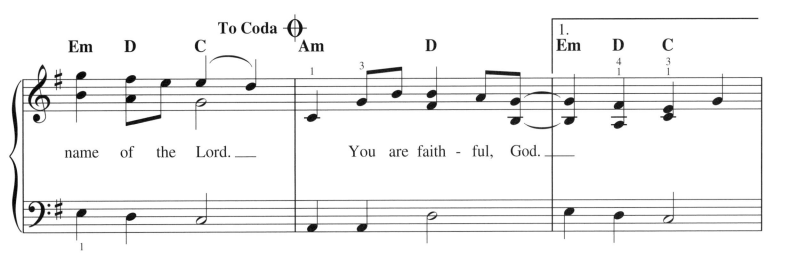

name of the Lord. _____ You are faith - ful, God. _____

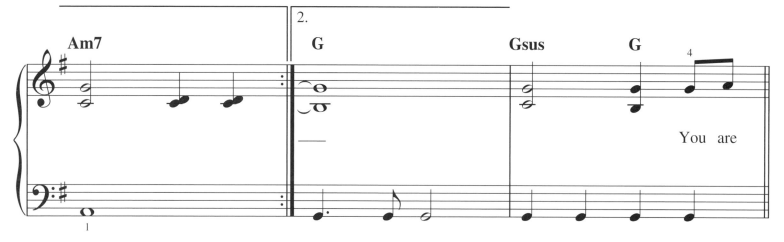

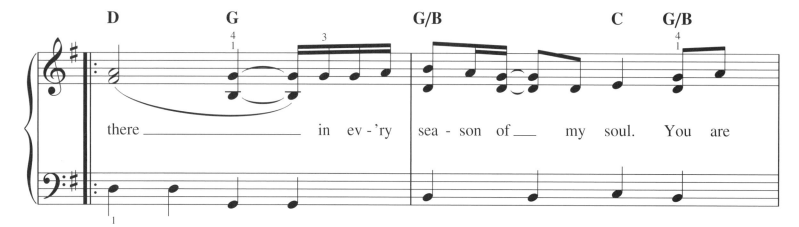

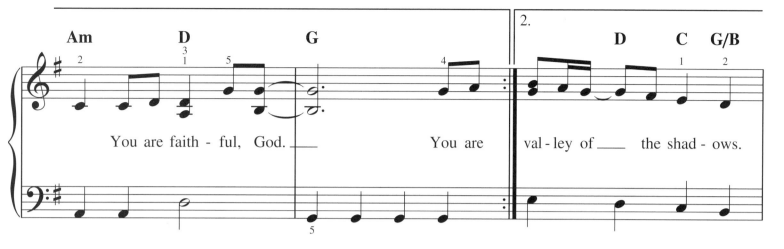

You are faith - ful, God. ____ You are val - ley of ____ the shad - ows.

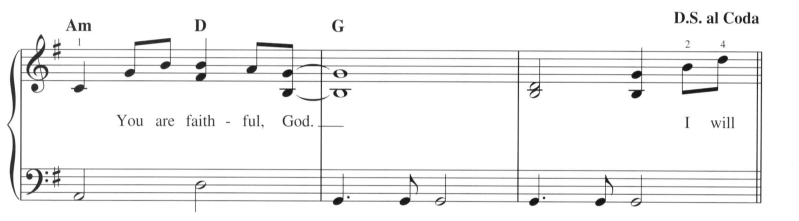

You are faith - ful, God. ____ I will

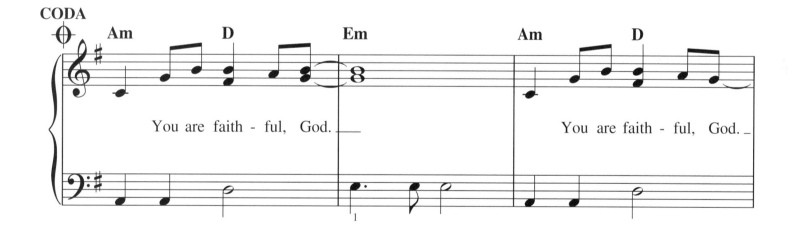

You are faith - ful, God. ____ You are faith - ful, God. _

____ rit.

LOVELY

Words and Music by CHRIS TOMLIN
and JASON INGRAM

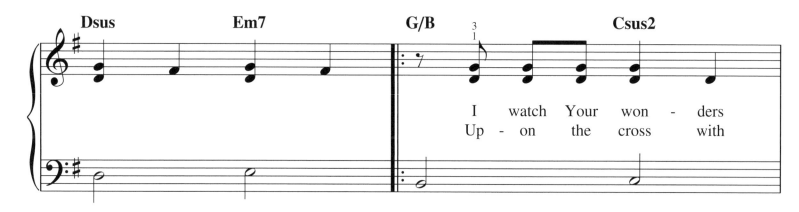

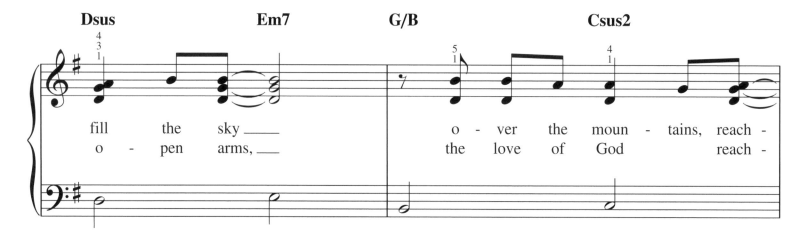

31

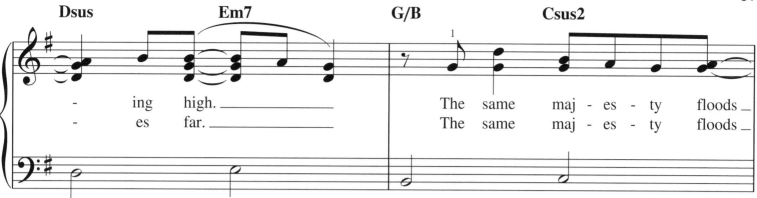

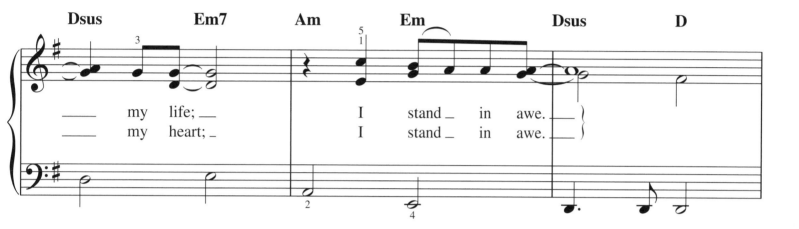

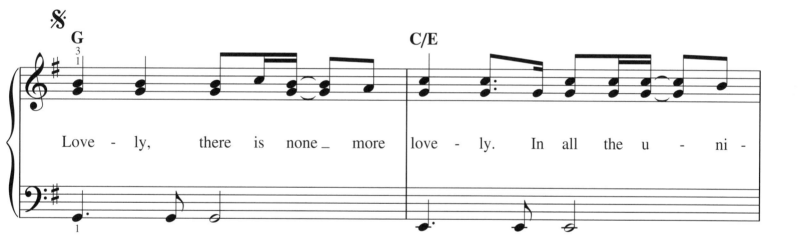

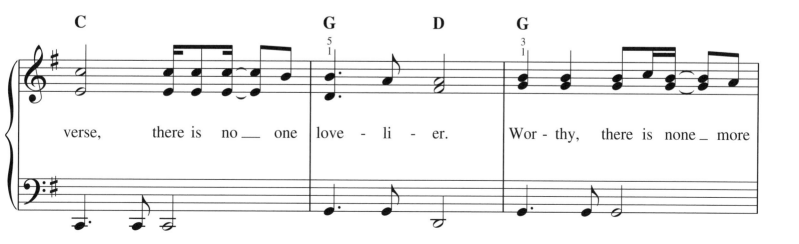

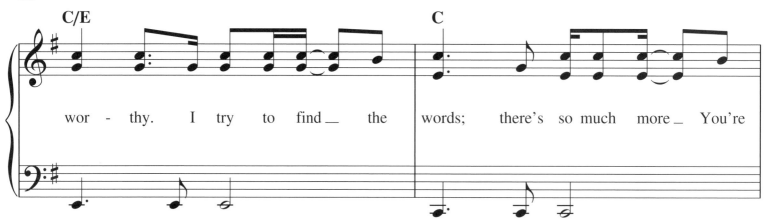

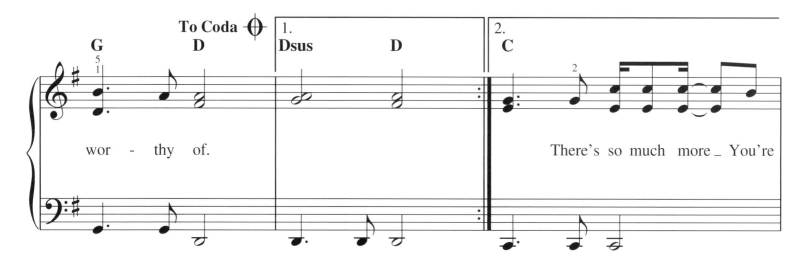

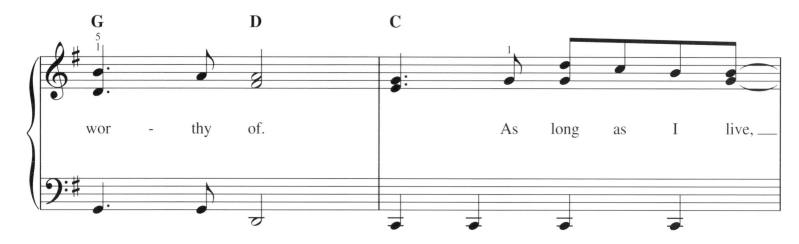

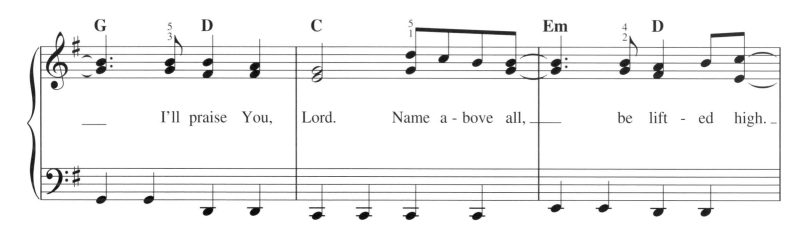

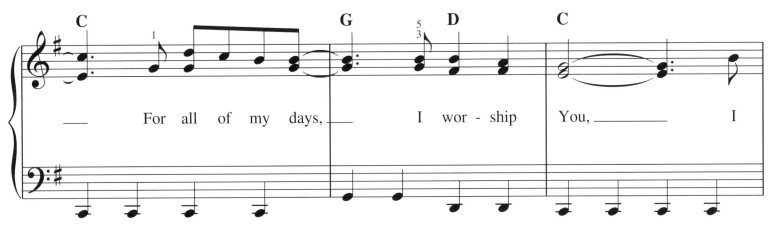

For all of my days, ___ I wor-ship You, _____ I

D.S. al Coda

wor - ship You.

CODA

There's so much more _ You're

wor - thy of.   There's so much more _ You're

wor - thy of.

THE NAME OF JESUS

Words and Music by CHRIS TOMLIN, JESSE REEVES,
MATT REDMAN, DANIEL CARSON,
KRISTIAN STANFILL and ED CASH

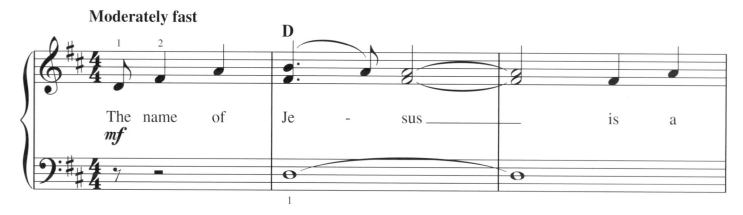

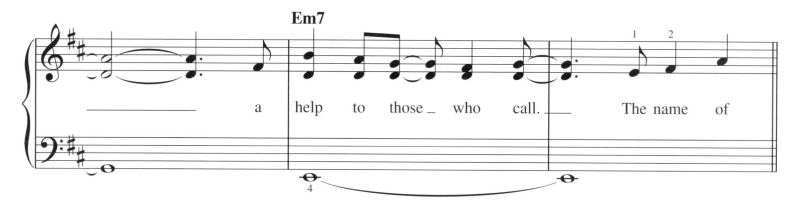

a sav - ing place _ to run, _____ a
Let all that You _ have made _____ bring

hope un-shak - a - ble. ___ When we fall, You are the Sav -
glo - ry to ___ Your name. ___

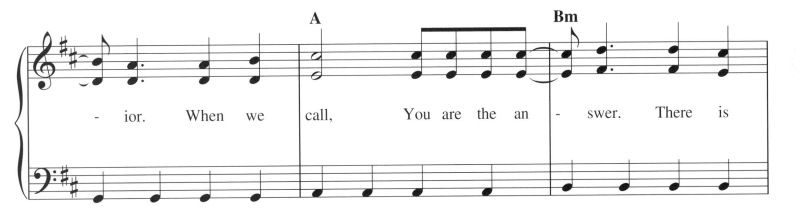

- ior. When we call, You are the an - swer. There is

pow - er in Your name, ___ there is pow - er in Your name. ___

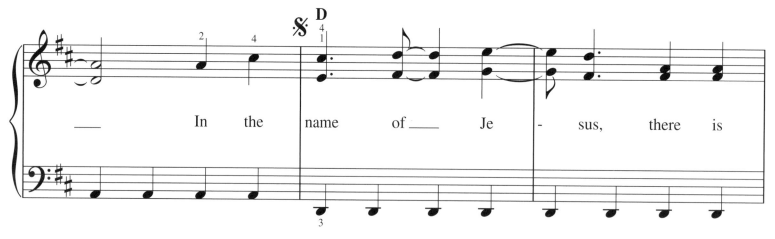

In the name of ___ Je - sus, there is

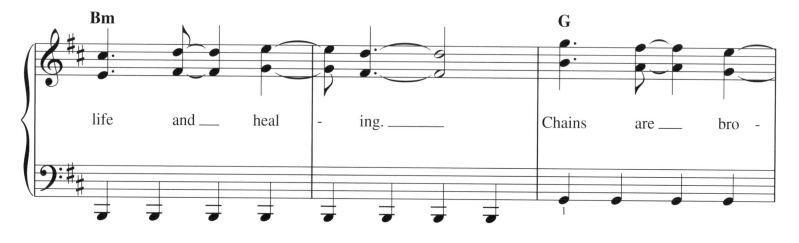

life and ___ heal - ing. ___ Chains are ___ bro -

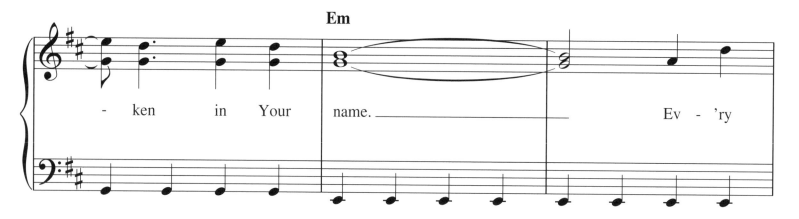

- ken in Your name. ___ Ev - 'ry

knee will ___ bow ___ down, and our hearts will ___ cry ___

out songs of ___ free - dom in Your

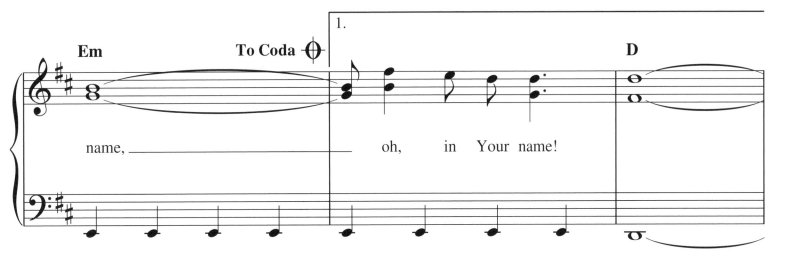

name, ___ oh, in Your name!

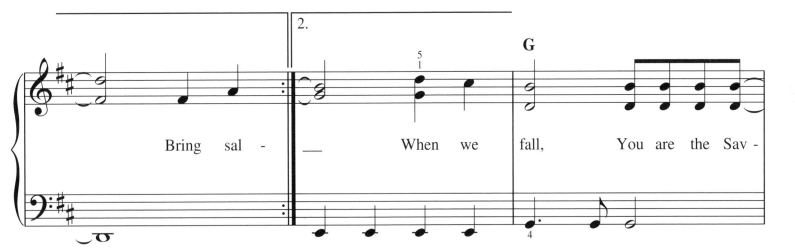

Bring sal - ___ When we fall, You are the Sav -

- ior. When we call, You are the an -

-swer. When we fall, You are the Sav - ior. When we

call, You are the an - swer. There is pow – er in Your name,___

___ there is pow – er in Your name.___ There is

pow – er in Your name,___ there is pow – er in Your name.

D.S. al Coda

CODA

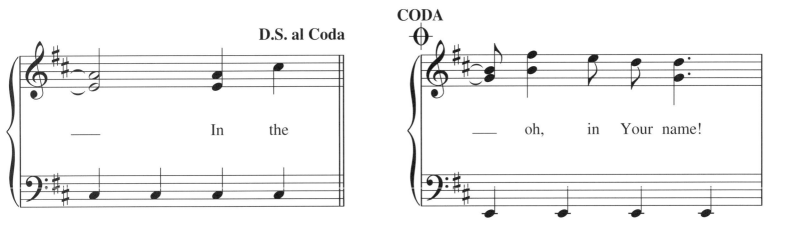

In the

— oh,   in   Your   name!

D

Bm7

G

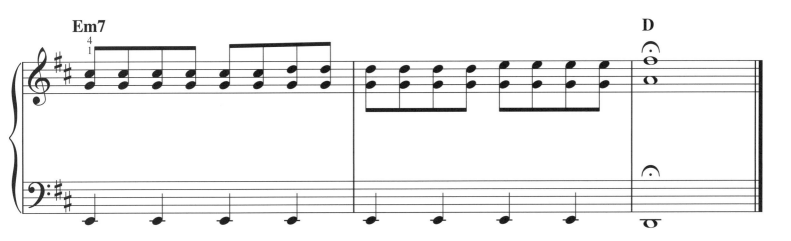

Em7

D

ALL TO US

Words and Music by CHRIS TOMLIN,
JESSE REEVES, MATT REDMAN
and MATT MAHER

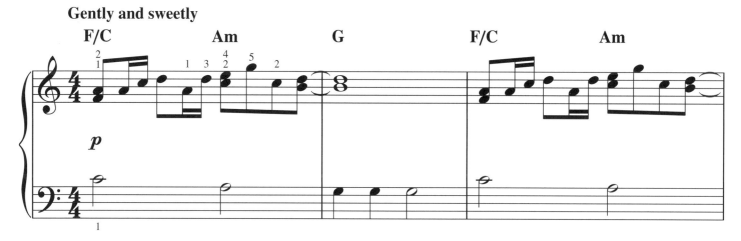

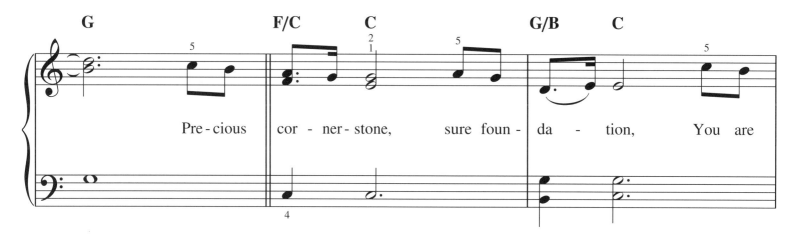

Pre-cious cor-ner-stone, sure foun-da-tion, You are faith-ful to the end.

faith-ful to the end. We are wait-ing on You,

Je - sus. We be - lieve You're all to us.

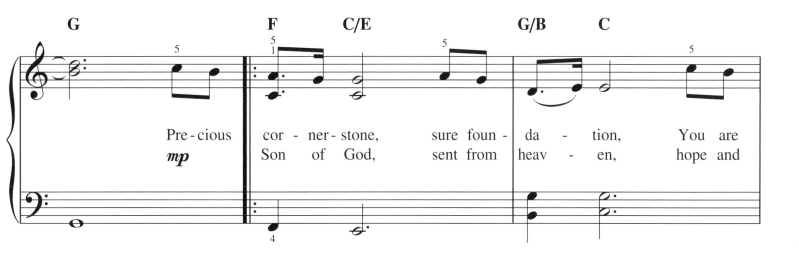

Pre - cious cor - ner - stone, sure foun - da - tion, You are
mp Son of God, sent from heav - en, You hope and

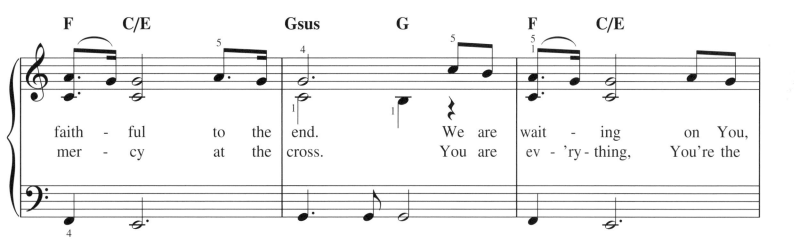

faith - ful to the end. We are wait - ing on You,
mer - cy at the cross. You are ev - 'ry - thing, You're the

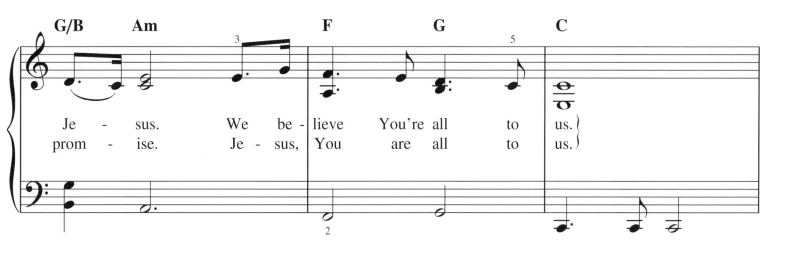

Je - sus. We be - lieve You're all to us.
prom - ise. Je - sus, You are all to us.

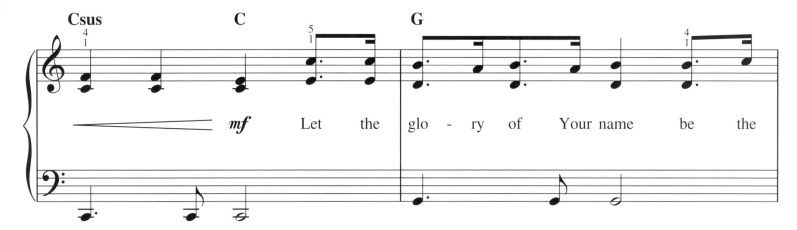

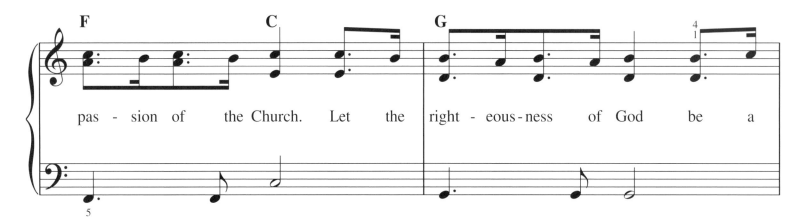

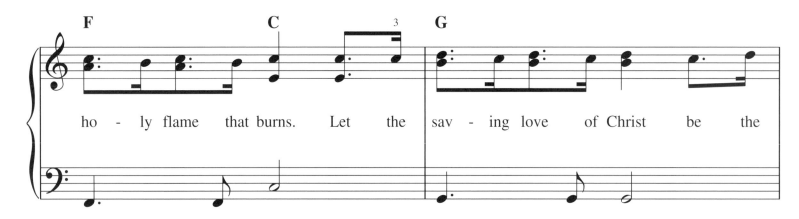

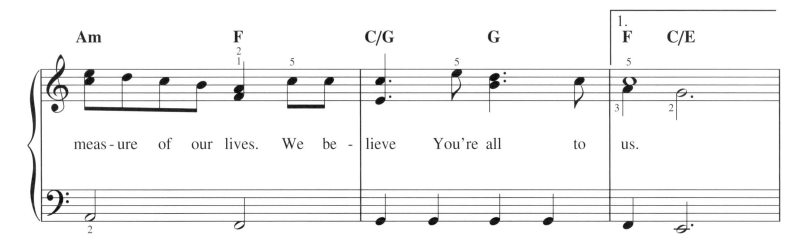

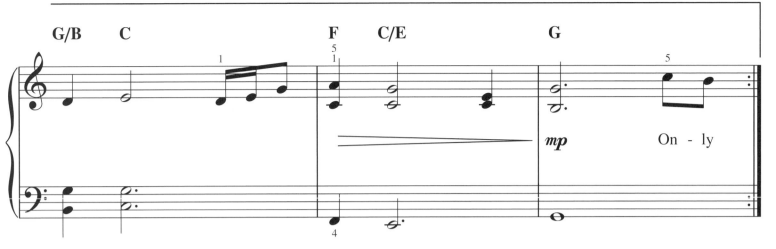

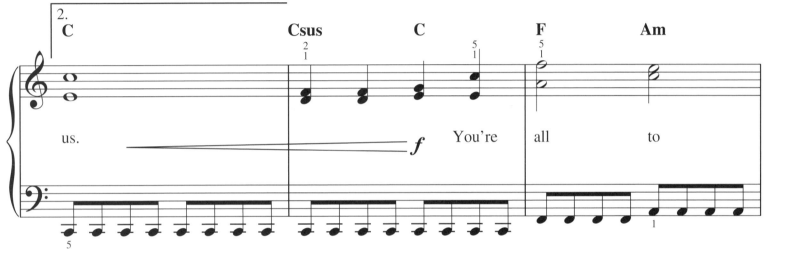

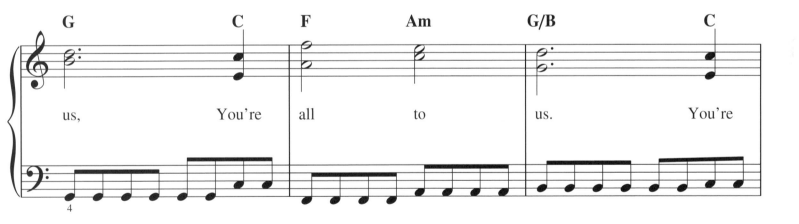

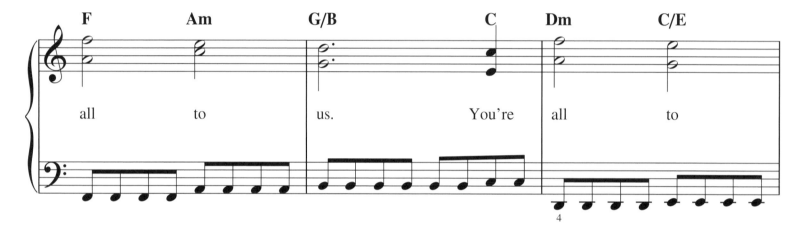

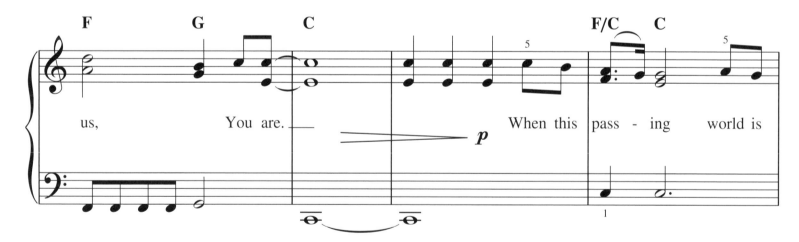

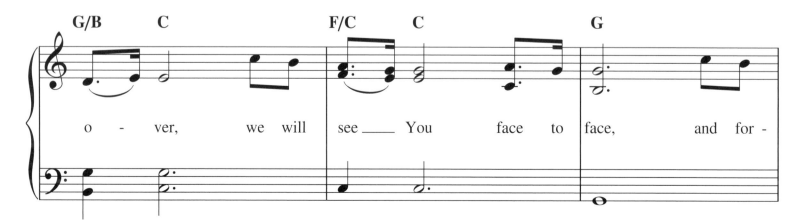

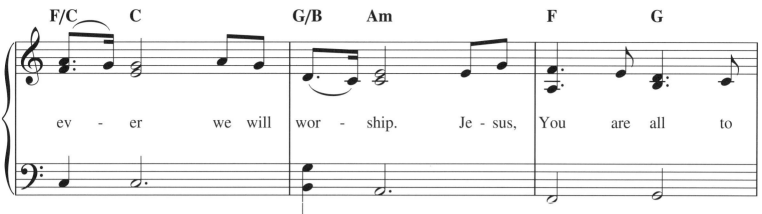

ev - er   we will   wor - ship.   Je - sus,   You   are   all   to

us.   Je - sus,   You   are   all   to   us.

You're ev - 'ry - thing   to

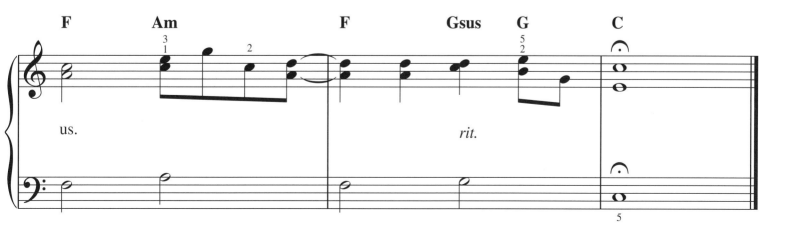

us.   rit.

AWAKENING

Words and Music by REUBEN MORGAN
and CHRIS TOMLIN

Worshipfully

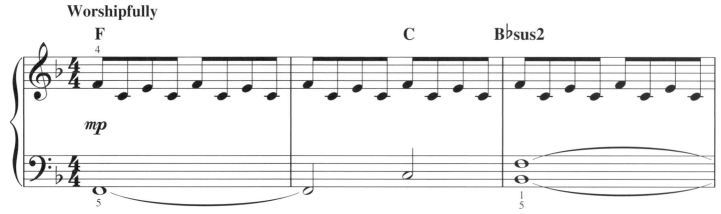

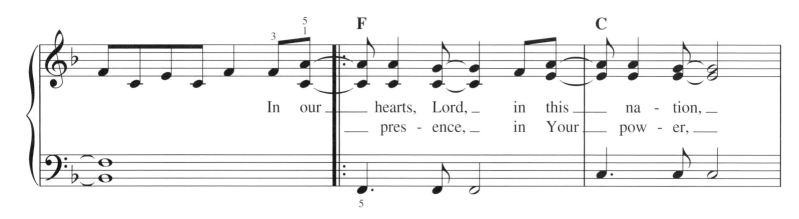

In our hearts, Lord, in this nation,
pres-ence, in Your pow-er,

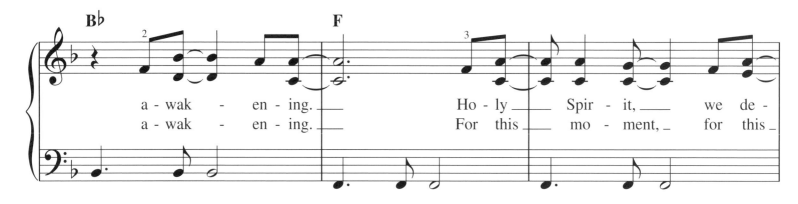

a-wak - en-ing. Holy Spir - it, we de-
a-wak - en-ing. For this mo - ment, for this

- si - re a-wak - en-ing.
ho - ur, a-wak - en-ing.

For You, and You a-lone, a-wake my soul, a-wake

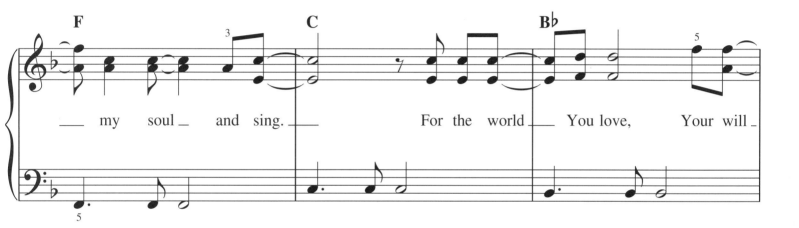

my soul and sing. For the world You love, Your will

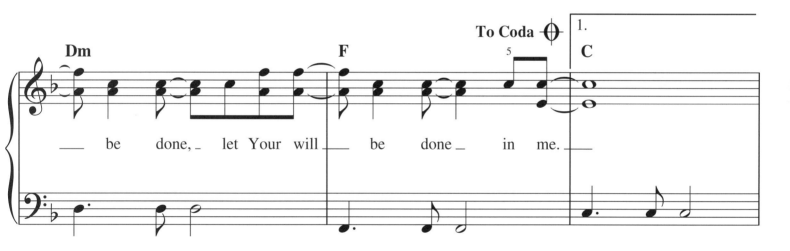

be done, let Your will be done in me.

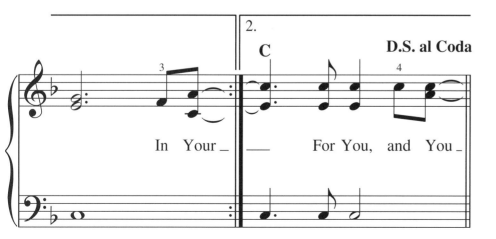

In Your For You, and You

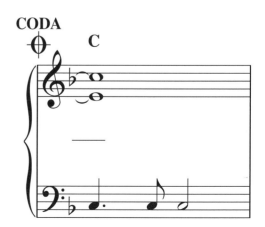

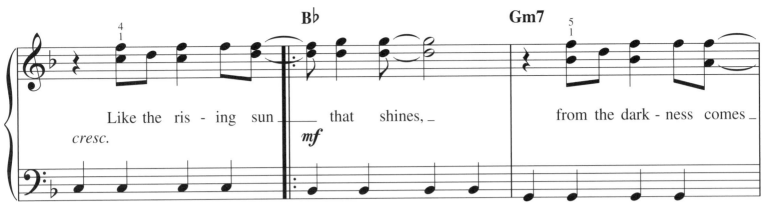

Like the ris - ing sun ___ that shines, ___ from the dark - ness comes ___

cresc.

___ a light. ___ I hear Your voice, and this is my ___

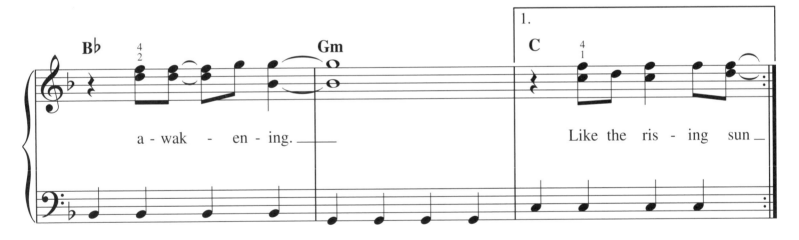

a - wak - en - ing. ___ Like the ris - ing sun ___

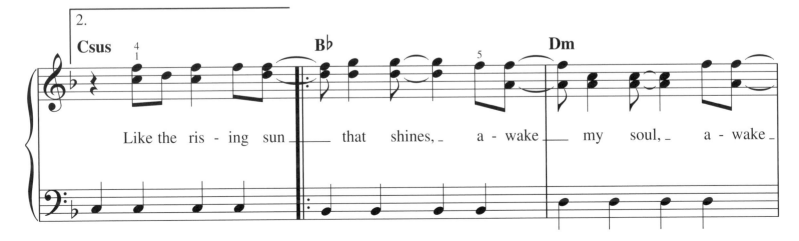

Like the ris - ing sun ___ that shines, ___ a - wake ___ my soul, ___ a - wake ___

my soul _ and sing. _ From the dark - ness comes _ a light; a - wake _
On - ly You can raise _ a life;

_ my soul, _ a - wake _ my soul _ and sing. _ Like the ris - ing sun _

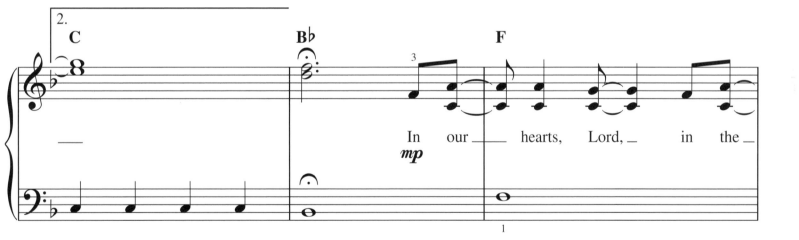

_ In our _ hearts, Lord, _ in the _

mp

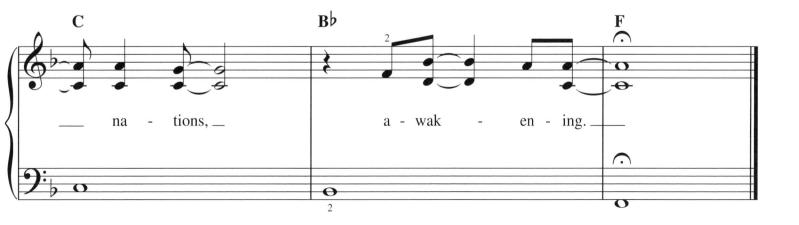

_ na - tions, _ a - wak - en - ing. _

JESUS, MY REDEEMER

Words and Music by CHRIS TOMLIN,
DANIEL CARSON and JASON INGRAM

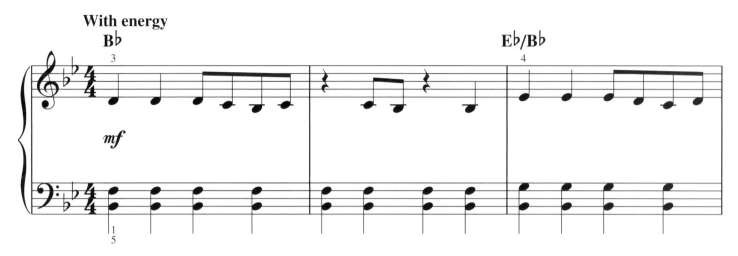

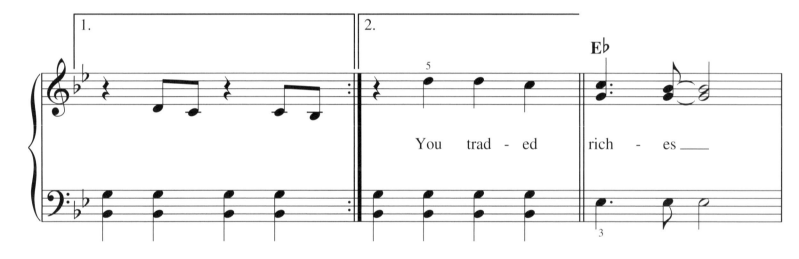

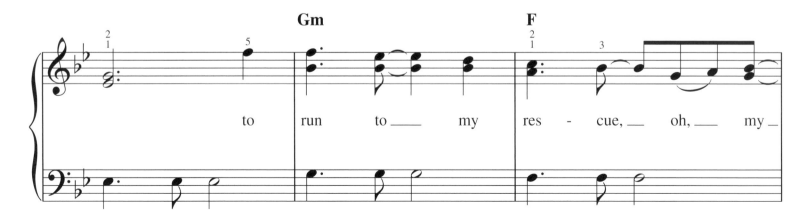

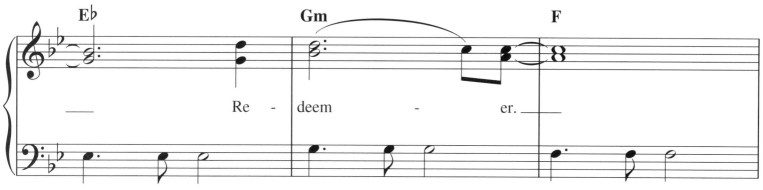

Re - deem - er.

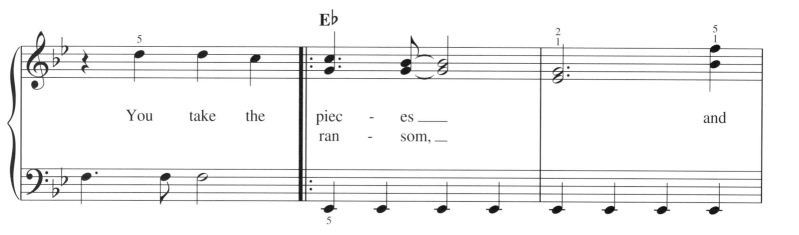

You take the piec - es ___
ran - som, ___

and

turn them ___ to prais - es, ___ oh, ___ my ___ Re -
You chose ___ to suf - fer, ___ oh, ___ my ___ Re -

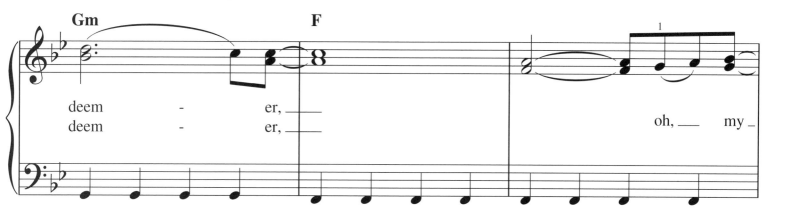

deem - er, ___
deem - er, ___

oh, ___ my ___

52

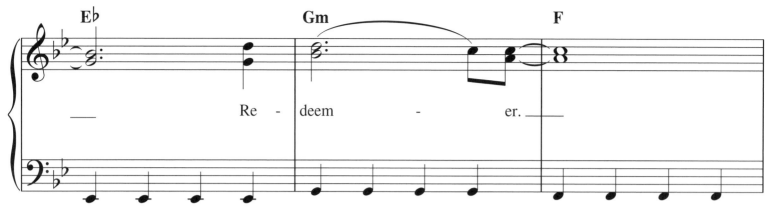

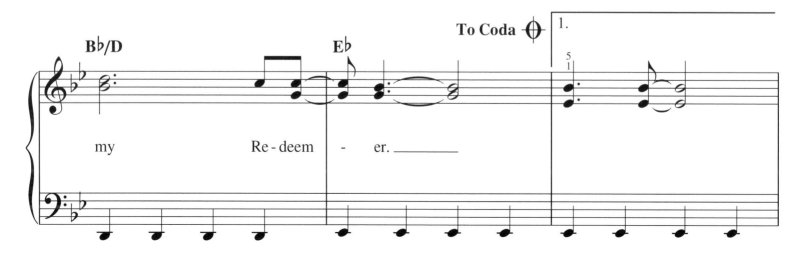

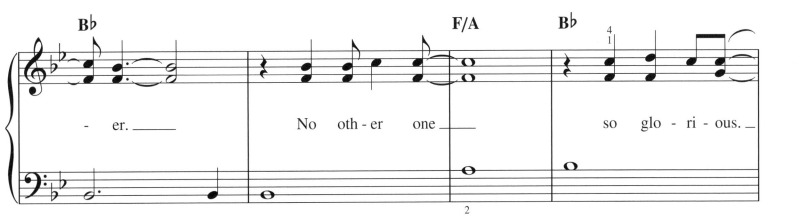

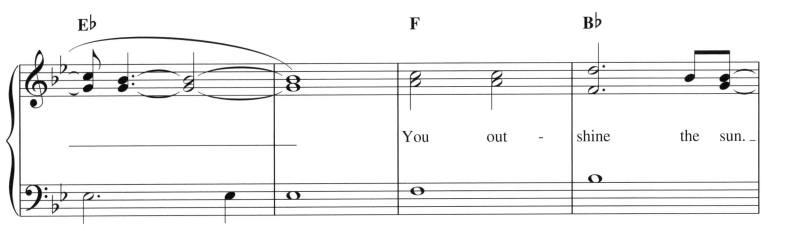

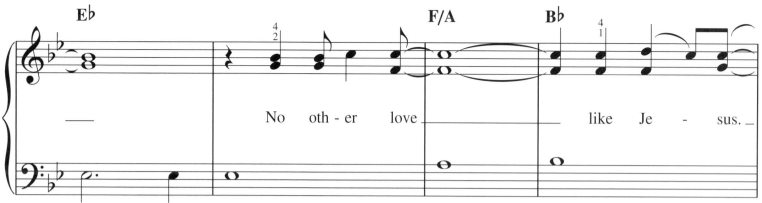

No oth-er love _____ like Je - sus. _

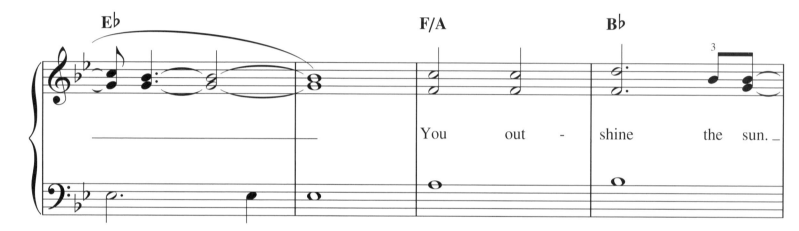

_____ You out - shine the sun. _

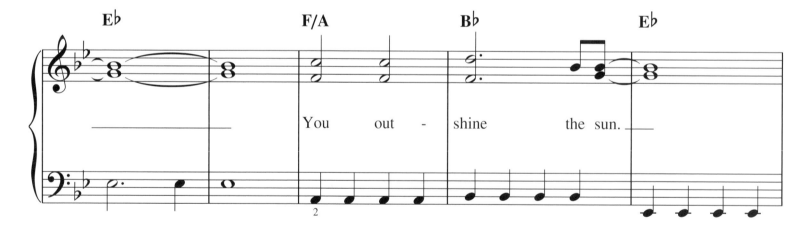

_____ You out - shine the sun. ___

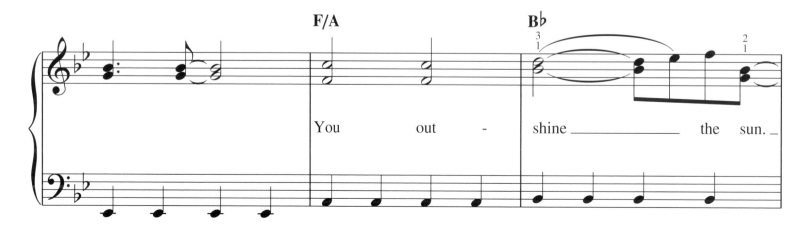

You out - shine _____ the sun.

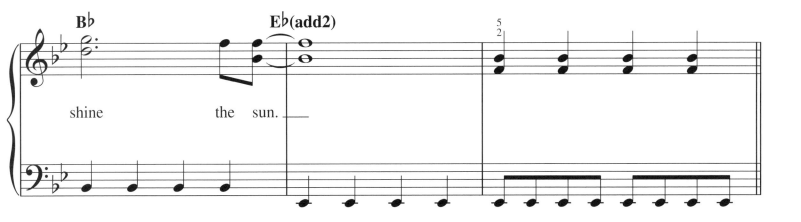

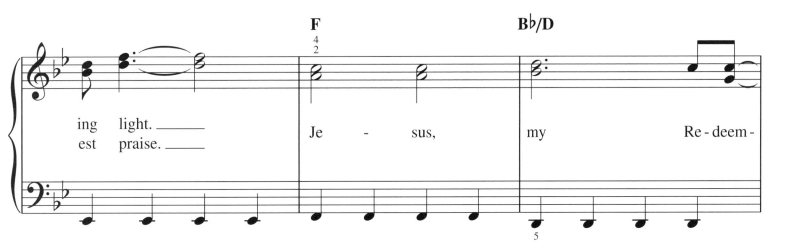

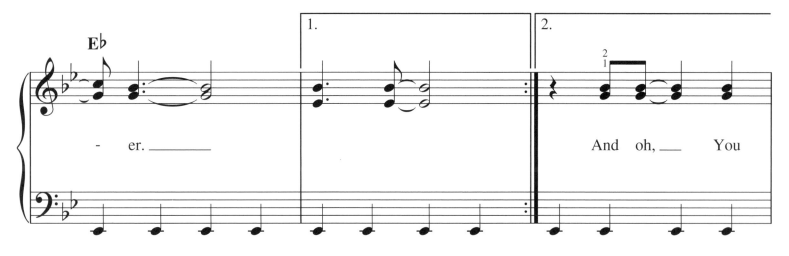

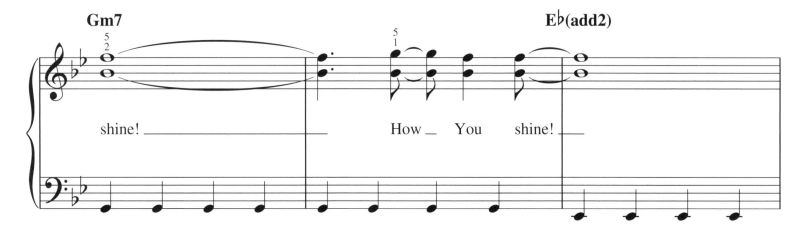

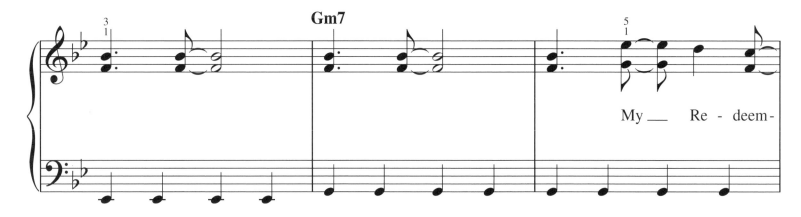